◀ **IN THE** Southwest, the Chihuahuan Desert crosses parts of Texas, New Mexico, and Arizona. The Sonoran Desert spreads over southern Arizona. The Colorado Plateau (left) is part of northern New Mexico and Arizona. Over time, wind and water have carved landforms into the plateau. A mesa is a hill with a flat top and steep sides. A butte (BYOOT) is a flat-topped hill that looks like a mesa, only smaller.

➤ **SO WHAT'S THE** weather like in the Southwest? Along the Gulf Coast, it is hot and humid, while mountain areas in the Southwest can be snowy in winter. But mostly, the Southwest is hot and dry. That's mainly because the mountains in the west stop wet ocean air from getting to the region. Still, sometimes desert rain showers come down hard and fast. When it rains, it really pours!

▲ **WHERE DO YOU** get water in such a dry region? In Arizona and New Mexico, people drill wells to get water from aquifers. An aquifer is a place where water collects underground. On large rivers, dams have been built to create reservoirs. A reservoir is a lake made by humans. Big pipes or canals called aqueducts carry the water to where it's needed. Built in the 1930s, Hoover Dam (left) is on the Colorado River. People use its reservoir, Lake Mead, for fun activities like waterskiing.

Early History of the Southwest

It's a hot summer morning in 1521, and you have a lot to do. You and your little sister go to the lake to get water. She's just old enough to do this chore. You have to help her keep the pottery jar on top of her head as you walk back to your village. You wave to your best friend, who's learning how to use porcupine quills to decorate the fabric her father wove. Later, you all watch the adults perform the Corn Dance. In one line, you see your father shaking a gourd rattle. In the other line, your mother carries pine branches.

In the 1500s, the Southwest was home to many Native American people. Some lived in pueblos, or villages, and were farmers. Not many trees grew in the desert. So, some of the people who lived there built houses out of mud, rocks, and adobe. Adobe is a mixture of sandy clay and straw that is formed into bricks and dried.

▲ THE PUEBLO people lived in the deserts of Arizona and New Mexico and mainly grew corn. The Caddo people lived in eastern Texas and Oklahoma. They also farmed, and their biggest crop was corn. But the Caddo didn't build adobe homes. Instead, they made big, dome-shaped houses out of tall pine trees and covered them with grass. Don't they look like giant beehives?

➤ OTHER NATIVE Americans in the Southwest did not farm at all. They were nomads, or people who move from place to place with no permanent home. The Apache were nomads who traveled around the region. They hunted deer and buffalo on foot. They ate the meat, sewed clothing from the skins, and made tools out of the bones.

▲ **THE PUEBLO**
people were known
for making pots
with interesting
designs. They used
the pots for cook-
ing and storage.
They also traded
them for other
goods. Hundreds
of years ago, some
Pueblo artists craft-
ed shiny black pots
with black designs
on them. In the
early 1900s, Native
American artist
Maria Martinez
figured out how to
make these pots.
Her black-on-black
pottery became
famous around
the world.

▼ **IN THE 1500s,**
Spain claimed most
of the land in the
Southwest. It built
forts to protect its
new property. By
1610, the Spanish
were building the
city of Santa Fe,
now the capital of
New Mexico. They
also built missions.
A mission is a reli-
gious settlement. At
missions, Catholic
priests taught
Native Americans
about Christianity
and Spanish culture.
Most missions had
a school, a church,
and workshops.

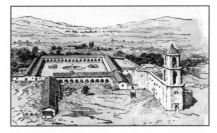

▲ **THE SPANISH**
often had little
respect for Native
Americans. Priests
made native groups
work on mission
farms and ranch-
es. They stopped
some people from
practicing their
own religions. Still,
the two groups
learned from each
other. The Spanish
brought in metal
tools, horses,
cattle, wheat, and
orange trees. Native
Americans taught
the Spanish how
to build with adobe
and use local plants
as medicine. They
also taught the
Spanish new ways
of watering crops.

Toward Statehood

It's 1830, and your family has been living in Texas for three years. The farm and fields finally feel like home, but sometimes you still miss your old house in Missouri. Then one night you hear your parents talking and wonder if you'll have to go back there. They're upset with the Mexican government, which rules over Texas. "First they raised our taxes," your father says, "and now they want to keep out all Americans!" Your mother says, "It's wrong, but what can we do?"

For more than 200 years, Spain ruled most of the Southwest region, including Mexico and Texas. In 1821, Mexico won its freedom from Spain and took control of much of the Southwest, including Texas. But settlers in Texas had come from many places besides Mexico. Most were from the United States. The Mexican government wanted to keep Americans from settling in Texas. First, it raised taxes in the territory. Then, it stopped letting people come in from the United States. Many people in Texas thought these laws were unfair.

▲ STEPHEN F. AUSTIN set up the first major colony of English-speaking people in Texas. He's known as the "Father of Texas."

After Mexico passed the laws to stop Americans from coming to Texas, he told other settlers, "We must defend our rights, ourselves, and our country." Soon, Texas and Mexico were at war. On March 6, 1836, at a fort called the Alamo, Mexican forces defeated a small group of Texans. But for Mexico, it was the beginning of the end.

➤ AFTER THE Alamo, Texans were even more determined to be free. On April 21, 1836, Texan soldiers took a larger Mexican army by surprise. The men ran into battle yelling, "Remember the Alamo!" Soon after, Texas won the war and became an independent nation, the Republic of Texas. In 1845, Texas joined the U.S. as the 28th state.

▲ **MEXICO OWNED** other parts of the Southwest, including the areas that are now Arizona and New Mexico. In the mid-1800s, President James K. Polk wanted the United States to become bigger. From 1846 to 1848, the two nations fought the Mexican-American War over those southwestern lands. After the U.S. won, many Americans moved west. Arizona and New Mexico became states in 1912.

▲ **IN 1830, THE** U.S. government decided Native Americans should leave their homes in the Southeast. It wanted them to move to what is now Oklahoma, which was then called Indian Territory. Many Cherokee refused to go. But in 1838, soldiers forced most of them to leave. More than 4,000 Cherokee died from sickness, cold, and hunger on the 800-mile trip. Their long journey became known as the Trail of Tears.

▼ **IN 1889, THE** U.S. government opened parts of Indian Territory to settlers. It offered land grants, or free land, to anyone who settled there. On April 22, 1889, the land grants began. At noon, officials gave the signal, and about 50,000 people rushed toward the land they wanted! Once again, land that was supposed to be for Native Americans became filled with settlers from the East. By 1907, Oklahoma was a U.S. state.

Mexican-American War

Texas has been its own country for as long as you can remember. But then again, you're only ten years old. Your big brother is 16, and he remembers when Texas was part of Mexico. Now, at the end of 1845, Texas has become the newest member of the United States. "Of course," says your brother, who likes explaining things, "Mexico doesn't approve of this at all." He says the two countries don't even agree about the Texas border. The United States says the border is a big river called the Rio Grande. But Mexico says the border is further north, at the Nueces River.

In January 1846, the U.S. wanted to meet with Mexico to settle their argument about the Texas border. The United States planned to offer up to $30 million for some of Mexico's land. But Mexico refused to talk about it. President James K. Polk sent about 3,500 U.S. soldiers to take over the area between the rivers. In April, Mexican troops crossed the Rio Grande and attacked those soldiers.

ON MAY 11, 1846, President Polk asked Congress to declare war on Mexico. In a speech to the representatives, he said Mexico had "invaded our territory and shed American blood on the American soil." Most of Congress voted to go to war. But some Americans didn't agree with that choice.

HENRY DAVID THOREAU

▲ SOME PEOPLE didn't want to go to war, because they were against slavery. They thought if the U.S. won, the Mexican lands would become slave states. Partly because of the war, author Henry David Thoreau wrote a famous essay, called "Civil Disobedience." It said people shouldn't always go along with the government's rules. If following the rules will make you do wrong, then it's right to break them.

◄ WHEN THE Mexican-American War began, California was ruled by Mexico. However, many Americans had settled there. In January 1847, military commanders on each side signed the Treaty of Cahuenga. Even though it wasn't a formal treaty between the two nations, it ended the fighting in California. Under the treaty, Californians got the same rights and privileges as U.S. citizens. Its signing set the stage for California to become a state.

THINK PIECE!
What do you think of Henry David Thoreau's idea?

United States, 1848

MEXICAN CESSION 1848

UNITED STATES

MEXICO

Rio Grande

Nueces R.

PACIFIC OCEAN

ATLANTIC OCEAN

Gulf of Mexico

N W E S

Scale at equator
0 — 500 mi.
0 — 500 km.

Treaty of Guadalupe Hidalgo boundary line
Present-day border

▲ **IN MARCH 1847,** American troops invaded Mexico, led by General Winfield Scott. He won victory after victory, capturing Mexico City that September. After that, the war was over. More than 10,000 U.S. troops died during the war, but most were killed by disease. Less than 2,000 died in combat. On the Mexican side, up to 25,000 troops and civilians died as a result of the fighting.

REENACTMENT OF THE SIGNING OF THE TREATY OF GUADALUPE HIDALGO

▲ **IN FEBRUARY** 1848, the Treaty of Guadalupe Hidalgo ended the Mexican-American War. Mexico gave up a lot of land, more than 500,000 square miles! The territory stretched from the Rio Grande to the Pacific Ocean and came to be known as the Mexican Cession. It included parts of what are now Arizona, New Mexico, Colorado, and Wyoming, along with all of what became California, Nevada, and Utah. The U.S. paid Mexico $15 million for the land.

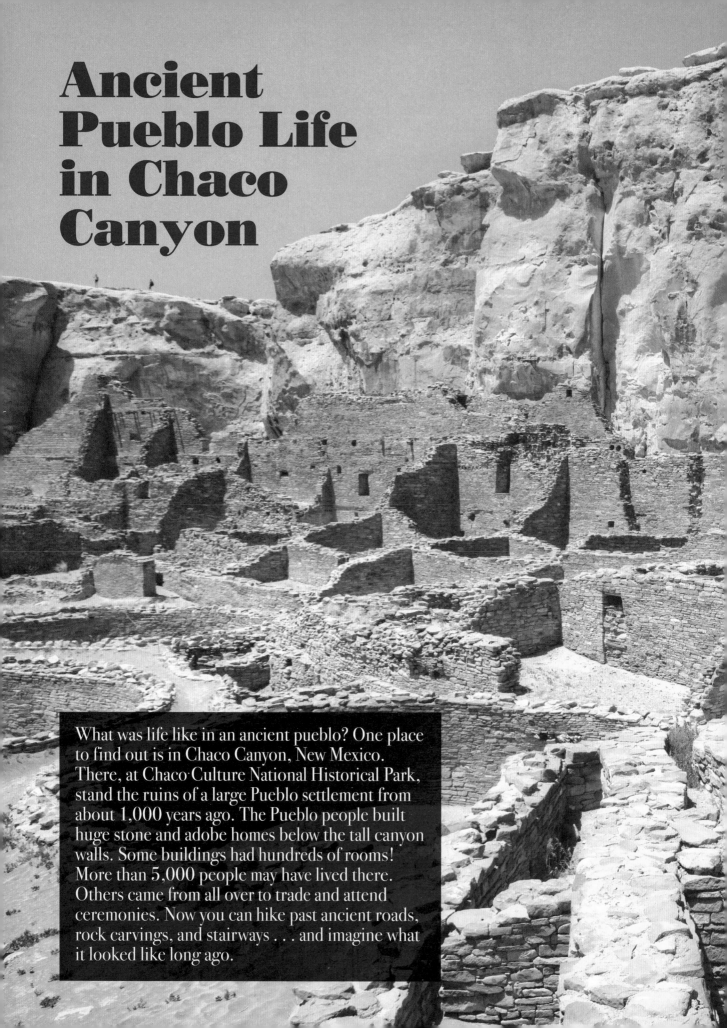

Ancient Pueblo Life in Chaco Canyon

What was life like in an ancient pueblo? One place to find out is in Chaco Canyon, New Mexico. There, at Chaco Culture National Historical Park, stand the ruins of a large Pueblo settlement from about 1,000 years ago. The Pueblo people built huge stone and adobe homes below the tall canyon walls. Some buildings had hundreds of rooms! More than 5,000 people may have lived there. Others came from all over to trade and attend ceremonies. Now you can hike past ancient roads, rock carvings, and stairways . . . and imagine what it looked like long ago.

Resources in the Southwest

It's just after recess, and the class is buzzing with excitement. You've been studying resources in your state, and you know a field trip is coming up. Today, your teacher will let everyone vote on where to go. You wonder what the choices will be. Maybe you'll get to see a cattle ranch or a solar power plant. Your best friend loves spicy food, and she wants to see a pepper farm.

The Southwest has many resources, and

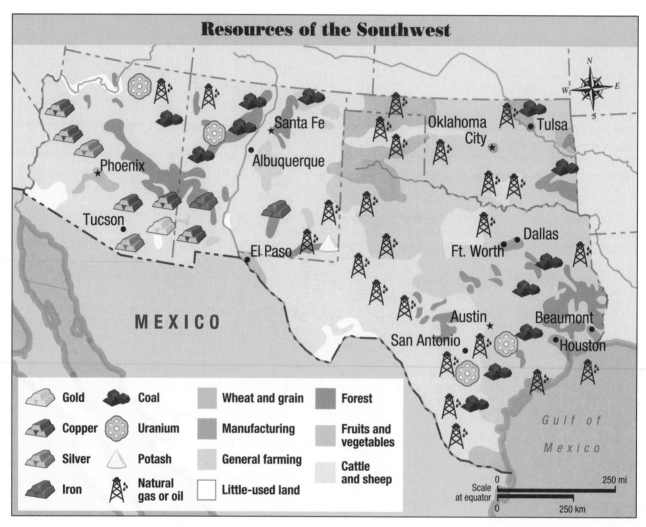

Resources of the Southwest

Santa Fe
Oklahoma City
Tulsa
Albuquerque
Phoenix
Tucson
Dallas
Ft. Worth
El Paso
MEXICO
Austin
Beaumont
San Antonio
Houston
Gulf of Mexico

Gold	Coal	Wheat and grain
Copper	Uranium	Manufacturing
Silver	Potash	General farming
Iron	Natural gas or oil	Little-used land

Forest
Fruits and vegetables
Cattle and sheep

Scale at equator
0   250 mi
0   250 km

◄ **MANY PLACES IN** the Southwest are arid, which means they don't get much rainfall. So, most farmers use irrigation to water their crops. Irrigation is the process of sending water to dry areas through canals, ditches, or pipes. It allows farmers in the region to grow many things. Their crops include cotton, wheat, vegetables, and citrus fruits.

people use them in different ways. They put cattle ranches on the grassy plains. They get pinewood from forests in northern New Mexico and Arizona. In eastern Texas and Oklahoma, they cut down oak and hickory trees, too. In Texas, Oklahoma, and New Mexico, people drill for oil and natural gas. They also mine coal, copper, and uranium. Uranium is a metal used as a fuel in some power plants. They also get energy from the sun to power homes and businesses.

▼ GRASSY LAND that's too dry for crops is great for ranches. In the Southwest, ranchers raise cattle, sheep, and goats. Early on, cowhands on horses moved cattle hundreds of miles to market. Would you believe it took only 12 cowboys to drive 2,000 to 3,000 cattle? Later, ranchers moved their herds by rail.

▲ AS MORE PEOPLE started ranches and farms, they needed more workers. But many jobs were temporary, lasting only until the work was finished. Migrant workers often did these jobs. A migrant worker moves from place to place, following the work. For example, a migrant worker might round up cattle in Texas, then head to New Mexico to harvest crops.

◄ THE SOUTHWEST'S booming oil industry began in the 1890s. In 1901, workers near Beaumont, Texas, found a huge oil deposit at a place called Spindletop. After that, thousands of people came to the region. They were all hoping to find "black gold." Cities like Dallas, Texas, and Tulsa, Oklahoma, got bigger thanks to the oil business.

THE RIO GRANDE is a major source of water in the Southwest. Its name is Spanish for "big river." The Rio Grande stretches almost 2,000 miles from Colorado to the Gulf of Mexico. It flows through mountains, canyons, and deserts. At Big Bend National Park in Texas, you can take a canoe trip down the river to explore its deep canyons. Keep an eye out for beavers, turtles, and colorful birds!

Texas and Oklahoma Today

The weekend is almost here, and you're ready to visit your grandfather's cattle ranch in Oklahoma. Your dad is excited, too. He loved his childhood on the family ranch. "I should have been a cowhand instead of a scientist," he says. You laugh, because he can barely stay on a horse now. You're a good rider, though, and he might even let you ride with the cowhands!

In Texas and Oklahoma today, people still farm and run ranches. However, most live in cities and work at newer jobs. Over the years, folks from all over the world have moved to these states. Along with large groups of European Americans and smaller groups of African Americans, Oklahoma has the nation's second-largest Native American population. Most live on a reservation, or land set aside for them. About a third of all Texans are Hispanic. Many Vietnamese people live in Texas, too. They moved there in the 1970s to escape war in their home country.

HOUSTON, TEXAS

➤ **MANY TEXANS** have jobs building aircraft and equipment used in air and space travel. Their business is called the aerospace industry. Astronauts train at the Johnson Space Center in Houston. That's also the home of International Space Station missions and other programs. Former U.S. astronaut Dr. Mae C. Jemison started two aerospace companies in Houston. She was the first African American woman to go into space.

▲ **ONE BIG INDUSTRY** in both states is food production. Texas has the most farms in the United States. Its ranchers raise more cattle than ranchers in any other state. Oklahoma is one of the top five beef-producing states. Its farmers raise huge crops of wheat, too. Many cowhands still use horses to round up cattle, but some use helicopters!

◄ **TODAY, TEXAS IS** the largest oil producer in the United States. Oklahoma and New Mexico are in the top ten. Some oil wells are on land, and others are underwater in the Gulf of Mexico. Crude oil, or natural oil, is pumped out of the wells. Pipelines, trucks, or ships take the oil to refineries like this one in Houston. A refinery is a factory where crude oil is made into products like gasoline.

➤ **HAVE YOU EVER** seen a bunch of windmills spinning close together on a hillside? That's called a wind farm. Texas and Oklahoma have a lot of wind farms. They're leaders in the industry of wind power. The wind turns the blades on a windmill, also called a wind turbine, and the turbine converts the wind's energy to electricity. The bigger the turbine, the more power it makes.

◄ **IN SPRING AND** summer, wildflowers make Texas more colorful. Texas-born Lady Bird Johnson was first lady of the United States from 1963 to 1969. She supported a program to plant flowers along the nation's highways. Native plants, she said, "give us a sense of where we are in this great land of ours." The city of Austin is home to the Lady Bird Johnson Wildflower Center. It works to conserve the state's native plants.

New Mexico and Arizona Today

It's your first trip to the Grand Canyon, and you are totally amazed. Your teacher taught you about this giant gorge in northern Arizona, but seeing it in person really makes you think. You look down toward the river on the canyon floor, more than a mile away. You remember learning about John Wesley Powell, who first explored the canyon in 1869. That was a long time ago, and Arizona has changed. But the Grand Canyon is as incredible as it was when Powell first paddled through in a wooden boat.

Arizona and New Mexico have grown a lot since Powell's time. Air-conditioning made living in the desert more comfortable. As more people moved to the desert, cities got bigger. The largest ones now are Phoenix (FEE-niks), Arizona, and Albuquerque, New Mexico. Highways, railroads, and airports make it easier to get around. People still work on farms, ranches, and mines in these states. But most have jobs in newer industries.

▲ **MANY ARTISTS** moved to the desert in the Southwest in the early 1900s. They liked its natural beauty – and the warm weather! Their artworks showed people what the region looked like. Georgia O'Keeffe (above) lived and worked in Santa Fe, New Mexico, where she painted pictures of the landscape. Artist Kate Cory lived on reservations. She painted pictures of the Hopi people and of the Grand Canyon.

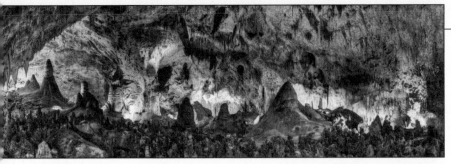

▲ **TOURISM IS A BIG** business in Arizona and New Mexico. People come from all around to see natural wonders like the Grand Canyon and Carlsbad Caverns (above). Visitors also like to explore the different cultures and historical places. Some might shop for Native American crafts in Santa Fe. Others might tour a historic Spanish mission in Tucson, Arizona.

▲ **EVER WANTED TO** see inside a volcano? You can do that at Capulin Volcano in New Mexico. Visitors drive along a winding road to the top of this extinct volcano. From there, they can hike on a trail around the rim or take a path down to the bottom. At the top of the 1,300-foot-high cone, you can see parts of four other states: Texas, Oklahoma, Kansas, and Colorado.

▲ **BOTH STATES HAVE** a lot of high-tech jobs. For example, many companies make electronic equipment and computer parts. Some New Mexicans work in the Los Alamos or Sandia national research laboratories. Some Arizonans work at the Kitt Peak National Observatory in Tucson (above). An observatory is a place where people study space with instruments like telescopes. Kitt Peak has 27 telescopes. It's the biggest collection of telescopes in the world!

THE ARIZONA TOWN of Fountain Hills has one of the world's tallest fountains. The water can gush up to a height of 562 feet. That's taller than the Washington Monument (555 feet)! Built in 1970, the fountain sits in the middle of a human-made lake. The town also has one of Arizona's largest collections of public art. It includes murals, sculptures, and more fountains!

Activities

CREATE A WATER CONSERVATION PLAN

Reread the parts of the magazine that discuss rainfall and water in this region. Think about what you and your family could do to use less water. For example, you could turn off the water while brushing your teeth. You could take shorter showers. Work with a partner to come up with a list of ways to conserve water. Share your list with others and compare ideas. See how long a list you can make.

WRITE A DIARY ENTRY

Suppose it's April 22, 1889, the day the land grants began in Indian Territory. Write a diary entry as one of the first settlers allowed to claim land there or as a Native American already living there. Explain what you saw, what you did, how you felt, and some of the hardships that you faced.

MAKE CONNECTIONS WITH THESE RELATED TITLES

The West

The West: It stretches from beyond the Arctic Circle to the Mexican border and from the Pacific Ocean to the Great Plains. It contains the highest and lowest spots in the country, as well as the biggest state and one of the smallest. Discover all that the West has to offer, from its breathtaking landforms to the amazing events in its history.

The Midwest

Find out why the Midwest is called America's "breadbasket." Which most important president was born in the region. And who we should thank for our automobile industry. Discover where the world's largest group of freshwater lakes is. What the name of the longest river in North America is. And why these geographic features are important for the whole country.

The Southeast

The Southeast is a region of firsts. The highest mountain peak east of the Mississippi River. The oldest continually occupied city in the U.S. The world's longest-known system of caves. The longest hiking-only footpath in the world. One of the world's most diverse ecosystems. Read about these firsts, plus the region's rich mix of people and culture and so much more.

LEARN MORE ONLINE!

- Many plants and animals in the Southwest have adapted to desert life. Black-tailed jackrabbits have big, thin ears that help them stay cool.

- The Republic of Texas was an independent nation from April 1836 to December 1846. In 1839, its capital city was named Austin, after Stephen F. Austin.

- For many American kids in the late 1800s, being a cowhand seemed like a great job. You'd be riding a horse all day and sleeping under the stars at night.

- People in Arizona and New Mexico are always figuring out ways to use less water. After all, they live in a very dry place! Many homes don't have grass lawns. Instead, residents use xeriscape (ZIR-uh-skayp), a way of designing a yard with rocks and desert plants that need little water.

Editor: Jennifer Dixon
Art Direction: Brobel Design
Designers: Ian Brown, Ed Gabel, David Ricculli, Jeremy Rech
Photo Research: Ted Levine, Sheila Sarmiento
Activities Writer: Marjorie Frank
Proofreader: Margaret Mittelbach
Fact-Checker: David Stienecker

Author: Natalie Nichols
Author Team Lead: Barak Zimmerman

President and CEO: Ted Levine
Chairman and Founder: Mark Levine

GRADE 4 TITLES

On the Cover: Cowboy on a horse overlooking Monument Valley. **iStock:** YinYang.

Picture Credits: Alamy: CSU Archives/Everett Collection: p.8 bottom left (Henry David Thoreau); Ian Dagnall: p.7 center (James K. Polk); Niday Picture Library: p.6 bottom left (Stephen F. Austin), p.9 top (U.S. Army capturing Mexico City); North Wind Picture Archives: p.4 bottom right (hunting buffalo), p.5 bottom center (Spanish mission); Pictorial Press: p.8 center (Mexican-American war); World History Archive: p.9 bottom left (Treaty of Guadalupe Hidalgo). **Bridgeman Images:** James Walker/California Historical Society Collections at the Autry/Mr. and Mrs. Reginald F. Walker: p.13 (cattle drive); Maria Martinez and Julian Martinez/Museum of Fine Arts, Houston, Texas, USA/Gift of Miss Ima Hogg: p.5 bottom left (jar with feathers and an avanyu); Tallandier: p.7 bottom (Oklahoma Land Rush, 1889); William Langdon Kihn/National Geographic Creative: p.4 bottom left (Caddos walk in their village of grass huts). **Getty:** Myung J. Chun/Los Angeles Times: p.8 bottom right (Treaty of Cahuenga); Time Life Pictures/The LIFE Picture Collection: p.15 top right (Mae C. Jemison); Tony Vaccaro/Archive Photos: p.16 top right (Georgia O'Keeffe). **Granger:** p.7 top right (Trail of Tears), pp.6–7 (Battle of the Alamo); Sarin Images: p.5 bottom right (Spanish explorer). **iStock:** 33ft: p.6 bottom right (Texas flag); Björn Alberts: pp.16–17 (Grand Canyon); Charles Schug: pp.2–3 top (hot air balloons); constantgardener: p.12 bottom (irrigated field); CrackerClips: p.13 bottom right (Rio Grande); hartcreations: p.15 bottom left (bluebonnets and Indian paintbrushes); mj0007: p.15 center right (wind farm); NNehring: p.13 top right (migrant workers); powerofforever: pp.10–11 (Chaco Canyon); RoschetzkyIstockPhoto: pp.2–3 bottom (Gulf Coast wetland); rwhaun: p.17 top left (Carlsbad Caverns); SeanPavonePhoto: p.14 (Houston skyline); Thomas Northcut: p.15 center left (oil refinery); zrfphoto: p.3 center left (Monument Valley). **Shutterstock:** Bill Florence: p.17 top right (Kitt Peak National Observatory); eatcute: p.18 top (water conservation); Irina Mos: p.19 top right (Savannah, Georgia); IrinaK: p.17 center (Capulin Volcano); Patrick Ziegler: p.19 top center (North Dakota field); ranchorunner: p.19 bottom (black-tailed jackrabbit); scullydion: p.3 bottom right (Hoover Dam); Sung Choi: p.19 top left (Oregon coast).

Original Illustrations:
Brobel Design: U.S. Map, pp.2, 9; The Albuquerque Box, p.2; Resources of the Southwest, p.12.

Michael Kline Illustration: Cartoons, cover; Cactus, p.3; Oil Rig, p.13; Helicopter and Cow, p.15; Fountain and Washington Monument, p.17; Role-Play Activity, p.18.

Wood Ronsaville Harlin, Inc.: Ron Spears: Corn Dance, pp.4–5.

Text Acknowledgements:
Quote "give us a sense of where we are in this great land of ours" by Lady Bird Johnson from the Lady Bird Johnson Wildflower Center. Text copyright © by Lady Bird Johnson. Reprinted by permission of the Lady Bird Johnson Wildflower Center.

Excerpt from *We Pointed Them North: Recollections of a Cowpuncher* by Edward Charles Abbott and Helena Huntington Smith. Text copyright © 1939 by Farrar & Rinehart Inc. Assigned 1954 to the University of Oklahoma Press. Reprinted by permission of the University of Oklahoma Press.

ISBN 978-1-328-81830-0

9 781328 818300

90000>

4

1687508